A Note to Parents and Teachers

Dorling Kindersley Readers is a compelling reading programme for children, designed in conjunction with leading literacy experts, including Cliff Moon M.Ed., Honorary Fellow of the University of Reading. Cliff Moon has spend many years as a teacher and teacher educator specializing in reading and has written more than 140 books for children and teachers. He reviews regularly for teachers' journals.

Beautiful illustrations and superb full-colour photographs combine with engaging, easy-to-read stories to offer a fresh approach to each subject in the series. Each *Dorling Kindersley Reader* is guaranteed to capture a child's interest while developing his or her reading skills, general knowledge, and love of reading.

The four levels of *Dorling Kindersley Readers* are aimed at different reading abilities, enabling you to choose the books that are exactly right for your child:

Level 1 – Beginning to read
Level 2 – Beginning to read alone
Level 3 – Reading alone
Level 4 – Proficient readers

The "normal" age at which a child begins to read can be anywhere from three to eight years old, so these levels are intended only a general guideline.

No matter which level you select, you can be sure that you are helping your child learn to read, then read to learn!

LONDON, NEW YORK, DELHI, PARIS
MELBOURNE, MUNICH

Project Editor Caryn Jenner
Art Editor Jane Horne
Senior Art Editor Clare Shedden
Series Editor Deborah Lock
Production Shivani Pandey
Picture Researcher Angela Anderson
Jacket Designer Karen Burgess

Space Consultant
Carole Stott

Reading Consultant
Cliff Moon M.Ed.

Published in Great Britain by Dorling Kindersley Limited
80 Strand, London WC2R 0RL
A Penguin Company

4 6 8 10 9 7 5 3

Copyright © 2001 Dorling Kindersley Limited, London
A Pearson Company

ISBN 0-7513-2910-X

Colour reproduction by Colourscan, Singapore
Printed and bound in China by L Rex Printing Co., Ltd.

The publisher would like to thank the following for their
kind permission to reproduce their images:
Position key: c=centre; b=bottom; l=left; r=right; t=top

European Space Agency: 19t, 20t, 29c; N.A.S.A.
24-25 background. **Eurospace Centre, Transinne, Belgium**: 6-7.
London Planetarium: 6. **N.A.S.A.**: front jacket, 4, 5, 8, 9tr, 9b,
10-11, 12-13, 14, 15, 16-17, 18, 26tl, 28-29, 31. **Planet Earth
Pictures**: 22-23, 22b. **Space and Rocket Center,
Alabama**: 24-25 foreground. **Science Photo Library**: 26-27.
N.A.S.A. Kennedy Space Center: front jacket, back jacket.
Paul Weston: illustration 30cl.
All other images © Dorling Kindersley.
For further information see: www.dkimages.com

see our complete
catalogue at

www.dk.com

DK DORLING KINDERSLEY *READERS*

BEGINNING
1
TO READ

Rockets and Spaceships

Written by Karen Wallace

DK
A Dorling Kindersley Book

5... 4... 3... 2... 1...
Blast Off!

Rumble... rumble...
ROOAAARRRR!
A rocket takes off
into the sky.
It zooms up and
away from Earth.

rocket

The rocket flies very far,
VERY FAST.

Rumble Rumble ROOAAARRR!

Rockets help us
to explore space.
Astronauts are scientists
who travel in space.

astronaut

They travel in a spaceship
at the top of a rocket.

The rocket takes
the spaceship up to space.
Then the rocket falls away.

Astronauts can see
the Moon and stars
in space.

planet

They can see
planets, too.
Our planet is called Earth.
This is how astronauts see Earth
from space.

Some astronauts have travelled
to the Moon.
They explored the Moon
and did experiments.

They picked up
dust and rocks
for scientists to study
back on Earth.

Sometimes, astronauts "walk" in space. Walking in space is not like walking on Earth.

Astronauts must use a special rope,
which keeps them
attached to their spaceship.
Otherwise, they would float away!

This is a space shuttle.
It is part rocket, part plane.
Astronauts have used it
for many trips to space.
The plane part of the space shuttle
can be used again and again.
It takes off like a rocket,
then it glides back to Earth
and lands like an aeroplane.

rocket
engine

The space shuttle uses
rocket engines to blast off.
When the rocket engines fall away
the shuttle plane flies into space.

A space shuttle does
many different jobs.
It can carry satellites
as well as astronauts.

satellite

Different kinds of satellites
do different jobs from space.
Special computers
help the satellites keep
their correct position
above the Earth.

The satellites send
and receive signals,
which help us every day.

Some satellites send signals from one part of the world to another.

We use these signals when we watch television or talk on the telephone.

Other satellites
take pictures
of the weather from
high above Earth.

This picture shows
a storm coming!

The Hubble
Space Telescope
is a very
special satellite.

It is a telescope
and a camera,
which can see
stars and planets
that are millions
of miles away.

The planet
in this picture
is called Saturn.

Saturn

Probes are machines
that explore space
on their own.
They do not carry
astronauts.

probe

Space probes visit planets
that are very far away.
They take pictures and
send them back
to scientists on Earth.

Mars

A space probe carried
this tiny buggy
to a planet called Mars.
The buggy explored Mars and
studied the rocks.

Some people think
there might be
life on Mars.
One day, scientists
will know for sure!

Some astronauts
stay in space
for months
and months.

The space station
becomes their home.
They do experiments
and learn about
living in space.

Imagine eating
and sleeping
in a place
where everything floats!

There are still so many secrets
to discover.
Scientists invent new rockets
and spaceships all the time.
There are even plans
to build a space hotel.

Greetings from **space**

Who knows?
One day **you** might go
on holiday in space!

Picture word list

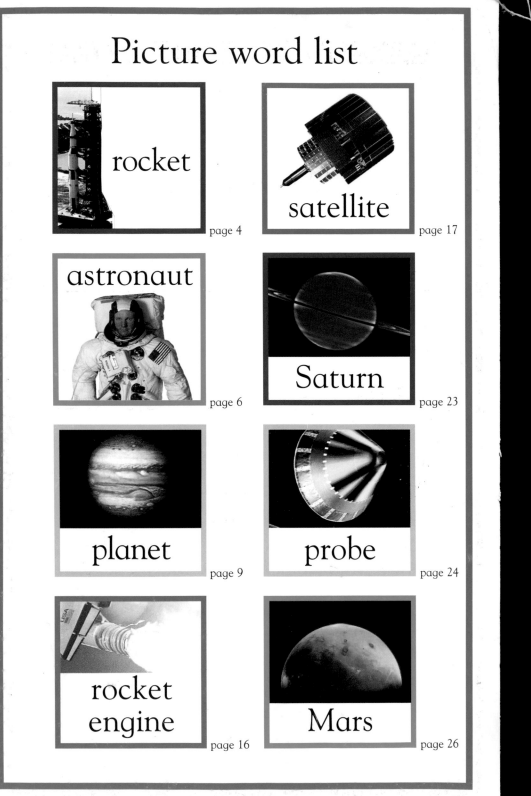

rocket

satellite

astronaut

Saturn

planet

probe

rocket
engine

Mars